WALKING
UPSTREAM

Men *in* Pain & How We Heal

Walking Upstream
Men in Pain and How We Heal

© Copyright 1997 by Scott D. Moore
   and Robert Brenning

Published by:
Crescent and Quill Press
232 Old North Shore Rd.
Two Harbors, MN 55616
(218) 834-4342

Quotation on page 42 copyright 1975
by A.J. McClane. Reprinted from
The Practical Fly Fisherman by A.J. McClane,
with permission of Lyons & Burford, publishers.

Printed in Illinois by Lithocolor.

10 9 8 7 6 5 4 3 2 1

Cover, cover illustration and book design by
Kollath Graphic Design; Duluth, Minnesota

Library of Congress in Publication Data
96-070848

ISBN 0-9651687-0-0

DEDICATIONS

To my wife, Tricia. I love you.
—Scott D. Moore

To my father, Abraham, strong and gentle.
Through his pain, he taught me how
to be a man.
—Bob Brenning

WALKING UPSTREAM

TABLE OF CONTENTS

WALKING UPSTREAM

PREFACE

This small book can change your life and the lives of those around you. Full of stories reflecting on the gifts of life, Scott and Bob remind us it is the journeys in life and not the destinations that are important. They ask us to search how we became men and how, as men, we deal with illness, crisis and loss. They remind us that ten percent of life is what happens to us and ninety percent is how we respond to it.

Full of wisdom, *Walking Upstream* shares the lives and crises of two men and those who care about them. It also allows us the opportunity to explore who we are now and who we want to become. Do we abandon old ways for new growth and new opportunities, or do we stay stuck in "that's how I was raised as a man and there is nothing now I can do about it"?

How do we change society's expectation that men be in control, be strong and be rational? Scott and Bob have given us tools to begin the process of exploring and discussing how men grieve, and how men grow. *Walking Upstream* reminds us to take chances in life and to reassess our priorities. It is about new beginnings. About opportunities during times of crisis. About hope!

> Ben Wolfe, Program Director
> St. Mary's Medical Center's Grief
>   Support Center
> Duluth, Minnesota
> Past-President, The Association for
>   Death Education and Counseling

INTRODUCTION

This book is by men, about men, and for men. It's for men who are suffering with a disease, or who have suffered with one, and are living with doubt and fear. This book is about struggling to go on in the midst of pain and worry. It's about grieving. Finally, this is a book about healing, finding resources in our male reality that give us courage and hope.

We authors came to this book with deeply personal but distinctly different perspectives. Scott Moore lives with the stark reality of eight years of cancer, of surgery and radiation. Bob Brenning teaches courses on grieving, dying and death, and he suffered the loss of his wife after sixteen years of cancer.

Thus this is a book of two views, two voices. Scott leads each chapter with a story drawn from his personal struggle. Bob follows with an interpretation based on a wider view that applies to other men.

We have found precious few books out there that are written in a straightforward manner specifically for men who are experiencing chronic or terminal illness. Our mission was to produce a handbook of help for men who are living with illness, pain, and grieving. We aim to help other men recognize that they are not alone in their feelings, emotions, and worries. Because we men traditionally have not been open in expressing what is going on inside ourselves, we tend to think that we are isolated, that we have no link with others who have gone through similar experiences.

So here is a beginning, a brief exploration, about male reality and illness, about grieving and hurting, about healing, about maintaining sanity amidst chaos. It is time that men feel free to talk, to express their feelings openly about hope and fear. To reach out to other men when all we feel is a terrible loneliness. To reach inside ourselves to learn about the power of laughter and humor in the midst of hopelessness and pain.

Essentially, what we are about, and what this book is about, is helping ourselves get through tough times with our sanity and souls intact.

Scott D. Moore
Two Harbors, Minnesota

Bob Brenning
Duluth, Minnesota

WALKING
UPSTREAM

Men in Pain & How We Heal

By SCOTT D. MOORE *and*
ROBERT BRENNING

CRESCENT
AND
QUILL

MEN AS GHOSTS

I was lying in my hospital bed, about a week after my surgery, when I realized that when people came in to see me they looked at me strangely.

I was white as a sheet, I was told. That was true. The color had been completely drained from my face and upper body. As I lay there, I noticed that people had many different reactions. Some were clearly in terror, actually becoming physically sick. Some cried, or would stay only a moment and then move on. Others came, recoiled, and immediately left, not to be seen again until months later.

I thought I made a good ghost, even if one less mobile than most ghosts. I will say this about my experience: There is tremendous power in being sick, though I perceived that my strength—once in my arms and legs— moved to my eyes and ears.

For the first time, I took advantage of the opportunity to observe people closely, and listen and see if all the data matched. It was true that I was vulnerable, but then so was everyone that came in my room. I was too weak to lift my head, with tubes hanging around me, and yet I could see through all

that to focus on people anywhere in
the room.

I had nowhere to hide, so my helplessness
led me to develop a new vision of myself and
opened a new avenue to communications
that lasts even to this day.

It took months for my color to come
back. It was not until four years later, when I
had been cross-country skiing for the first
time and had come into my home and
looked in the mirror, that I finally saw color
in my cheeks, a smile on my face. I was back.
The ghost was gone.

As in Dickens' famous *A Christmas Carol*,
I was given the opportunity to watch myself
from a ghostly distance. I carried that
perspective with me through the surgery and
treatments and into the next stage of my life.

We do have special powers when we are sick.

*When we are sick we have the power to
manipulate. Not only loved ones, but doctors
and nurses. Something dreadful is happening
in our bodies. We are the center of a great
deal of attention.*

*Our world can get small and even petty. We
can order people around, get angry over the*

slightest things, and play with the emotions and guilts and shames of those we love.

But this power can take a positive form. We can make sure that we are included in all treatment decisions, everything having to do with our bodies and minds. We are, after all, the star of the drama.

A second power is the nurturing kind. This is a word we as men are not accustomed to using in connection with ourselves. Because of how we were brought up, following the models of man that so many of us had, we left the nurturing to women. But nurturing can be an important part of who and what we are as men.

When we are sick, for a short or long term, we have people around us constantly who are concerned, who are hurting in their own ways. In quiet ways we can be of help to them and in the process take a vacation from our illness for awhile. To listen, to ask the probing question, to talk through someone's resentments with you, to help someone you love hear that that love is returned—all these are nurturing actions, and they have tremendous healing powers.

A third power is that of observation. When we are in the midst of fighting a disease or illness, we have a unique perspective. We are on the inside of the illness, looking out. No one else has that view of reality.

Just as we are vulnerable in illness, so are many of those who care for us. Employing the power of observation gives us insights we might otherwise never have gained into their inner selves, into what makes them laugh and hurt, what makes them uncomfortable, what gives them hope. This and more we can see through that special vision we have when we are on the inside looking out.

When we are ill, we have a special stewardship of certain powers that can benefit ourselves and others. What we learn about those powers can benefit us well into recovery and beyond.

I THINK I CAN

When the kids were young, the distant sound of Duluth Missabe and Iron Range Railway locomotives starting their climb along Minnesota's famed North Shore of Lake Superior and past our home was our cue to pile the family in the car and hustle off to catch the train somewhere along the ridge on Five Mile Hill.

Up on the ridge we could get to within thirty feet of the massive engines and feel their awesome power. The kids would hide behind me as the engineer sounded the clamoring horn. We would wait for the last car to go by, savoring all the sensations, before turning around and slowly heading home.

After my cancer treatment, the outings took on new meaning. I would chase down the trains to stand by the rail bed and feel the force of the diesel-electric engines. They embodied sheer strength, each engine generating one thousand horsepower. Think of that—three thousand horsepower!

I came to realize that none of the engines by itself could do the job. One thousand horsepower wouldn't even budge the load.

The trains were about a mile long. It took three engines to get them to the top of Five

Mile Hill. Every once in awhile they would stop halfway up the grade, almost as if pausing to call a meeting to say, We're not together on this one; let's try it again.

I had a load of cancer cells. I paused on the tracks, checked the load, gave it a good effort—and nothing happened. I needed a team, with the right attitude, pulling in the same direction.

I wasn't the first man to miss that point when sick and vulnerable. I don't know why. Back in the old logging days, no one tried to use a two-man crosscut saw by himself. And it takes five to run an effective chase team in competition biking, eight or nine to paddle a North Canoe, fifteen to twenty to crew an America's Cup boat. Why not rely on a team with cancer?

My load was a long one. I made it heavier by failing to realize the power of engines in tandem. I came around because I had no choice. Later I would marvel that the team approach was working as I watched the last cars crest the hill and drop out of sight.

One of the more destructive characteristics of men growing up in our culture is the way we have insisted on being the strong, silent type. Too many of us learned from our fathers and other role models that the way to be a man is to never ask for help, never cry, never let anyone see that we are hurting or scared.

When we are sick or fighting a disease, we are more vulnerable than usual to fear. But if the only response we know is to draw inside and conceal our emotions, we miss out on incredible help that can come from others.

We also set loose a bunch of volatile emotions that can make crazy things happen. One of the many rotten results is isolation.

But when we begin to share what's going on inside of ourselves with someone who cares and knows how to listen, all the stuff that is circling around in our heads—fear, panic, and anxiety—begins to look different. It is as though all the things banging around inside us begin to line up in a neat, orderly fashion. We can sort out the crazy thinking from the sane. We begin to see more clearly what it is we need to concentrate on.

We need others to help us make it. It's that simple—but also that complicated. Complicated because we are not normally

accustomed as men to being open to someone
else when we hurt.

So we have to learn a new behavior. We
have to risk that the person we are sharing
with will not reject us.

Opening up may feel awkward at first. That
is normal. The key is to find someone you
trust. Reveal just a little at first. Test the
waters. Then risk a little more. You will
discover that sharing your burden with
another makes it easier for you to pull
that train.

CHECKING IN

When I was a kid, I'd check in for hockey tryouts, school and summer camp. I checked into college (and out again, too many times). Checking in at airports and motels became a routine part of my business life.

Once, during a winter break long before I was sick, I checked in at the trail head for a hike along the Pigeon River at Grand Portage, in northern Minnesota. I read the register of names of others who had made the winter trek earlier and marveled at their toughness.

It was fifteen degrees below zero. The river was frozen. Nothing was moving. I saw no tracks, no birds. I was the only living thing on the river. Everything else was frozen in white.

The temperature reached thirty below that night, one of the coldest of my life. I made it through the night but was more than ready to leave on the following morning, cutting my stay by a day, thankful that I was alive and warm. I gladly checked out.

Two years later, I checked in for another journey. This time the trail head was at the entrance of the Mayo Clinic. Again the dominant color was white: coats, floors, dishes, walls. The difference was that I was not able to check out at my discretion. I was the one that was cold and frozen; everything around me was alive and moving.

The bigger difference was that when I checked in, I thought that maybe I was the only one to have taken this path. As I found out, thousands of people had gone before me. Greg, my key caregiver, urged me on. Shayna, a clinical nurse specialist, kept me focused on my goals. People pushed me to higher levels.

It was clear that only by reaching out could I succeed. My wife duked it out with the head doctors. My mom babied the nursing staff. Together the team got me down the trail.

All my life I had chosen to go it alone. Now, how different my life was as I was compelled to let others pull for me. I was weak and fragile. But at the end of a dark, cold night, I was full of life and ready to check out.

Several times in this little book, we talk about reaching out for help. There is a good reason for this. As men, we have been taught to keep everything inside us, to be self-sufficient. The message seems to be that a

*real man is a self-contained entity. And that
is baloney.*

*We need other people just as we need food
and water. Without sustenance we die on
the inside.*

*In times of crisis, however, we often seem to
retreat into ourselves at the very time when
we need most to lean on others. Stubborn as
we often are, proud when we least need to
be, we deprive ourselves of help by a
misguided sense of self pride.*

I think of Lean on Me *as a good theme
song for us in our crisis. Leaning on others
when we need to has nothing to do with
being less of a man; it has to do with the
recognition that we are human underneath
all the gender stuff. We hurt, cry, and suffer
just like everyone else. We are not different.*

As a good friend once told me, "Come on,
just join in. Become a common turd like us.
Let us help!"

*Those words aren't particularly elegant,
but they are wise.*

SCARS

I grew up playing hockey in northern Minnesota. Most of the players had scars of one sort or another. My buddies were proud of their battle wounds.

After seventeen years of playing I had got away with only a stick or two to the chin and that was it. But my surgery left me with close to thirty inches of scars. My kids called the scars on my back railroad tracks and were always asking when would they go away.

I became self-conscious about my scars, aware of them no matter where I went. At the same time, I kept thinking that I should be proud of them—they were signs that I had made it through.

My scars cut to the heart of who I am. On my left shoulder, my scar was fat and short. Another, on my left leg, was long and thin. My back was full of staple marks. I felt like a slave with my history stamped on my back.

My scars were visible, easy to follow along the map of my journey. Your mental scars from chemo or radiation therapy are just as real and just as revealing. I found that by sharing my scars, I shared myself.

All of us have scars. We also have stories go with many of them, and sometimes we love to share those stories. They re-create an important time in our lives.

We also have emotional scars. Just as our external, physical scars point to experiences that were painful at the time, so it is with our internal scars.

I have a memorable scar on the inside of my thigh that came from leaping—or trying to leap—a barbed wire fence in hip boots while trout fishing. The leap was motivated by stepping on a rattlesnake. How I got over that fence I will never know—but I did it.

I also have internal scars from watching my wife put up a very long fight with cancer. I have scars from the hurt I caused myself and others by becoming an alcoholic.

Scott has thirty inches of scars on the outside and yards of them on the inside. So do you. And I. They are a table of contents to our lives. Scars help us tell stories about ourselves. And what are stories? Sometimes they are medicine. They help us heal.

CHOICES

Until I had my cancer I never thought too much about the choices in my life. I had a lot of practice, like most men. My job demanded that I make choices and decisions that sometimes involved other people and their livelihoods.

Hunting and fishing choices were easy and fun. Most of the time I chose the correct grouse of a pair to swing on first for a double. I cleverly determined whether to take a north fork or south fork in a stream, and which fly to select.

One time years ago I chose to walk through miles of grizzly bear country with an eight and a half foot graphite rod looking for fifteen-inch flaming red cutthroats. Best decision I ever made, though not without some fear and second-guessing.

I could look back and feel that many of my decisions were good ones. So I took my history of decision-making into the Mayo Clinic. Now I was playing with the big boys—and my life.

Some of my choices were somewhat irrational.

I decided in thirty seconds that this surgeon was for me. Why? Because he kept his hands perfectly still. He wrote his notes in the most beautiful handwriting I had ever seen.

And I decided that I would go for it all: surgery, radiation, and then a life after. Without a full regimen, I was guaranteed a life of disability. That was not for me. Even with the full regimen, I faced the possibility of dying a horrible, slow, painful death, or living life as a paraplegic. I had made up my mind.

I came out of my treatment a poor specimen: beaten up, weak, confused, and frustrated, but still determined to continue to make my own decisions about my care, my life.

We take pride in most of our choices, even when we make bad ones and have to work through the negative consequences to gain fresh perspective on what we learned. Our lives are an amazing jigsaw puzzle of choices and decisions. But we have made it this far, and gained some wisdom.

Even when we are in the middle of disease, with our world in chaos, we constantly have to make choices. If we don't decide, others decide for us. Now is the time to trust what we have learned through earlier decisions.

"Go with your gut." We've heard that phrase often, and even though as men we are often told that we are out of touch with our feelings, there is a core part in all of us that we have learned to trust.

In the middle of treatment decisions, in the whirlwind of frightening new knowledge and lots of questions from others, we need to continue making our decisions for ourselves and our bodies.

It is a deep affirmation of who we are as human beings to retain the right to decide what will happen to us.

BAPTISM

When I was diagnosed with cancer, in 1989, our children were three and two years old.

I had been to church a couple of times. I didn't look good. I was so white. All those people had been praying for me. I had a friend who they prayed for and she died. I hoped they wouldn't pray too hard for me.

On one big day for our family, we went to church for Patrick and Keihly's baptism. I had a cane and was sick to my stomach, with a spasm raging in my back. I couldn't carry Patrick. (It would be years before I could pick him up again. The first time I did it, I looked into a face that showed utter surprise.)

But we made it to church that day, and during the service we proceeded to the altar, each parent holding a child's hand, each child holding a candle. Patrick started trying to blow out his candle. Here I was trying to keep my candle—my life—lit, and he was trying to blow his out.

His life, so new, was free from worry. Mine was lost and coming apart. His hands were warm; mine changed from boiling hot to

frigid cold every fifteen minutes. It was a
wretched morning in a miserable life.

I asked many times after that poignant day:
"Would I go through my cancer again for
Patrick and Keihly?" The answer was
always yes.

*Look at all the men in the suicide statistics
and you come up with quite a study. Young,
old, retired, prime of life, sick, healthy, every
profession. We make up quite a list.*

*In the middle of our battles with disease,
dangerous thoughts flit through our minds.
Sometimes they last only an instant; other
times we play with them a bit.*

*Can I make it through this thing I'm
fighting? What will I look like? What will I
still be able to do? It would be a relief from
the pain—physical and emotional. I wouldn't
be a burden to my family anymore. What is
the easiest way? The most painless? The
least messy?*

*Is this crazy? Not at all. There are times in
our battles with disease that inevitably such
thoughts cross our minds. This is human.*

But as typical males, we tend to keep all this locked up inside and dig ourselves even deeper into the pity trap. Fortunately we do have ways out.

A few years ago the politicians took over the phrase "points of light" for their dark purposes. We need to take the phrase back and use it to help ourselves. Where are the points of light in our lives? The smile of a child, a magical cloud formation, the sound of wind in the trees, the smell of fresh-cut grass, a visit from a friend, a sentence out of a book, a word spoken by a loved one—these are all points of light, if we let them be. Often the choice for life comes down to holding on to one or more of these little sparks.

Yes, desperate thoughts cross our minds at times. But we have choices about what to do with those thoughts. Life is about decisions, and looking for the light.

ZERO GEAR

Before I was sick, I enjoyed riding bicycles. They were geared for my active life, but not for my cancer.

After cancer treatments, it took me about four years to be comfortable enough to start exercising again. I had not accepted my new self. I felt fragile. My legs were weak. I could walk well, but I was no longer the athlete I had been.

At some point, I decided to try riding bicycles again. I bought a Trek cross trainer with 21 speeds thinking that would cover all the bases. The first thing that I noticed was the damage to my left leg, the result of surgery. With part of the muscle lining gone, it lagged behind the rest of me. The brace slowed my pace. I was reminded constantly of my cancer. Clearly this would not work.

It became obvious that my goals needed to change. Obsessions about time and speed and distance yielded to being thankful that I could simply participate.

My bike had all the best features, like the grip shifts that let me focus on pedaling, not shifting.

There was, however, one item my bike didn't have—a gear lower than low, something for the hardest pull: Zero Gear.

Kringle Hill was where I especially needed it. It started steep—first gear. It flattened out for a few feet and then climbed again, even more steeply than at the start.

I had no gear for this upper section. Legs flailed, arms failed, back and lungs screamed, "Stop, I want to get off."

I couldn't see the top. I kept my head down, searching for the strength to make one more turn of the pedals.

Somehow I learned to make one more turn, take one more day, one more step, one more treatment at all costs with no memory of how I got there or how it happened. I had found Zero Gear—my legacy from cancer.

Today is all we've got. So our disease, our operation, our recovery is not going well, and has got us feeling down. Maybe we need to kick into a lower gear and start taking things as they come, a minute or an hour at a time. We need to just get through this moment, this particular piece of pain. We grit our teeth and do it.

I remember the days of driving a grain truck in the wheat fields of North Dakota. When my truck was fully loaded, I would shift into super low and, at two miles an hour, power my way out of the field with engine screaming, springs groaning, tires half flat from the weight.

Sometimes we need to imagine ourselves in super low gear, enduring our way through the next step, feeling all the aches and pains, hearing ourselves groan—knowing that this minute is all we've got. We have to power through it, reach down deep inside, and realize that the very act of doing so is also a part of what it means to be human.

We may not want to dig deep down. We may want to escape the pain—physical, emotional and spiritual. But this is our present. Yesterday is gone, tomorrow isn't here. It is in getting through the tough moments that we make our victories.

In a paradoxical way, it's when we accept our suffering and pain in all its agony and hurting that we gain the courage for the next struggle. Gearing down to super low, to Zero Gear, is what courage is all about.

TOUGH

I thought I was pretty tough when I was a kid. I took notorious Jap Portage—520 rods—in the Boundary Waters Canoe Area in one shot not letting the canoe touch the ground until the end. I jumped from eighty-foot cliffs into deep clear water. It was not uncommon for me to double-pack and put a canoe on my shoulders just to see how far I could go.

Once, while hitch-hiking from Minneapolis to New York City, I waited for a ride on the south side of Chicago for eight hours. On that same trip I slept in a halfway house sound as a baby and never worried about tomorrow or what it might bring.

I found out in 1989 what tough really meant. As they wheeled me down to therapy in a wheelchair I was crying. Every little bump set my back into spasms. I was dizzy, and disoriented. I was in the depths.

When I got down to therapy, I was put to work near another patient, a woman in her late sixties who had an artificial leg. I watched her struggle through the parallel bars. She was in obvious pain, and she was working desperately. Compared to this, Jap Portage was a stroll in the park.

She made little progress. She kept on trying anyway.

From that point on, my attitude toward therapy changed. I realized that others had gone before me, and as Maureen Fell Pierson said in her book *Measuring My Days*, "The way to the sunrise lies that way, at times the path is narrow, rough, and steep; at times it opens up, widens out as a gentle slope reaches a new level."

I wasn't as physically rugged in those days of therapy as when I was a kid. But inside there was a new steel born of tempering and time. I had learned that others suffer and yet endure to forge a new day. I had learned what being tough is all about.

Men in or culture learn how to be tough at an early age. We get the messages about toughness almost by osmosis. They are in the air we breathe.

But what does being tough really mean? When we are ill, when our cancer, when the radiation or chemotherapy is hurting like crazy, what does our learning about being tough say to us? Not a whole lot.

We need to redefine toughness. Real toughness is in the letting go of the superficial appearance of strength. Real toughness is the ability to affirm our continuing survival even in the middle of a terrifying illness.

Getting tough means developing callouses on the inside of ourselves so that our capacity to fight increases when disease is getting us down, when things look hopeless, when we feel depressed, when recovery seems distant and the pain is so immediate.

Real toughness means living the best way we can today.

THE RISK

I was sitting in my brother's rustic outpost cabin. It was November; 10 to 15 degrees above zero; snow and cold. I was up in the North Country hunting whitetails. I realized that it could be the last time I would ever hunt. My legs were weak, and I dared not venture far in case they gave out.

I put another log on the fire and sat back to think that maybe this was what the explorer Robert Falcon Scott experienced at the South Pole.

Scott's journal told of the heroic effort he and his men made, though in the end they failed. Scott's last night must have been horrible. He was all alone, with nobody to share his thoughts or fears.

I sat on the bottom bunk, left side—mine since we started hunting. I had a date on the next day with my neuro-orthopedic surgeon. I knew that I could come out a paraplegic, or not at all. I wondered if I would make it back.

As a male, I went through the waiting with the typical stiff upper lip, but I was learning what true fear is. It is knowing that you are part of an event that you no longer have control over.

Scott was a hard driver like myself. He was energetic, a leader, intelligent, and a risk taker. And yet, there he was, huddled in his tent, maybe the last person in his group alive, wondering where he had gone wrong, going over and over his failure until his last breath.

In cancer, too, it is cold, dark, and silent.

Here I was, though, at the cabin, and ready to risk sharing my fear and pain.

The fire crackled. My brother approached and stamped the snow off his boots on the porch.

The coffee was perking, and if I didn't share my thoughts then, I would not be able to bear the moment alone as they gently put me to sleep.

When tomorrow faces us with a test of our whole being, we feel so alone. This is a pain and suffering that stretches us almost to the breaking point. As men, we often withdraw into ourselves so completely at those times that nobody can get in. And, often, we need to do this for awhile to muster all our resources in order to face the test that is coming. But after the gathering up of our courage is done, then we need to reveal how scared we are.

We don't find this easy to do. It goes against the grain of what we've learned a strong man is all about. Or so we think.

Now is the time, however, to risk being so strong that we can share how truly deep our fear runs, how we shudder with it in the middle of the night, how the quiet tears overwhelm us behind closed doors.

Giving ourselves permission to share our pain and fear is so difficult to do, and yet is what makes us truly human. To share our sense of powerlessness over what is going to happen tomorrow can even give us a sense of control again. That is the paradox of the giving of ourselves. We also receive.

HELLO, TOES

I woke up a week after surgery to a beautiful sensation—I could feel my toes! Yes!

You made it! You are alive! Celebrate!
Give thanks to whatever higher power is
yours to thank!

Breathing—it's good to breathe!

Hurting—yeah, it hurts, but it means
I'm alive!

Hoping—I've got a future!

Smiling—well, maybe just on the inside.
Because it hurts to stretch my mouth.

BEGINNING WITH
THE END IN MIND

I stopped to rest in the warming shack after struggling around the cross-country ski trail. A couple of people had passed me. I don't like getting passed but, after cancer and surgery and treatments, just being out on the trail was good enough.

While warming up, I browsed through a magazine and found an article about two men who had skied across the Sierra Mountains unassisted. They were paraplegics. Neither of the men had any use of his legs, and here they were cross-country skiing.

Shortly before going to Rochester for surgery, I had taken some time off for a hunting trip and a little solitude, and to shore up my emotional self.

As it turned out, that was a good place to start, because weeks later, after surgery and radiation, there was little left of my physical self.

One day I grabbed my wife by the lapels and screamed at her that she didn't understand. My sanity was slipping away. Realizing that, finally, I went into counseling and started to sort it out.

I would learn that maintaining a grip on sanity is a process, a journey just like life. Nobody, no thing, and surely not cancer, would take my sanity away from me.

It was time to put another log on the fire to keep the hut warm. Then it was time to step back into my ski bindings and try skiing again. If those two guys in the Sierras could make it, so could I.

Some days, in the middle of illness, we feel like we are going crazy inside. Our bodies have let us down. We don't know if we have the reserves left to stay sane.

A lot of us have learned only a couple of ways to deal with these feelings, and they are not necessarily healthy.

The first is to turn our anger inward on ourselves.

Or we direct our anger outward toward those who are closest to us: our wives, children, caregivers.

There is but one way to deal with this frustration on our bad days: Take it an hour at a time.

But what we do with each hour, what we fill it with, is very important. Down deep there is a wild man in all of us. Getting in touch with that wild man can help us find our sanity. We need to remember the times we have howled at the moon (maybe we were drunk—but so what?), or the weird chances we took when we were younger and thought ourselves immortal.

When we are feeling crazy, we may need to crawl deep inside ourselves and then come back out to the surface, recognizing that maybe it would be smart to talk to someone about how and what we are feeling.

We know that as men we're not very good at this talking stuff.

But our sanity is worth saving—even if it means we have to talk about it.

GRIZ

My dad hunted big game all over North America—everything from moose in Alaska to jaguar in Mexico. A story that he told over and over was about his grizzly bear hunt in British Columbia.

He and his guide had come upon an elk carcass that had been fed upon by a bear. It was on a small knoll, surrounded by dense brush on all sides, with no vantage point. They considered waiting for the bear even with the problem of an uphill shot.

After some discussion they decided they would wait it out.

The bear eventually showed up and started to feed on the carcass. Because my dad was below the bear, all he could see were its shoulders. That's where his first shot hit.

The grizzly stood up to its full height. My dad then put three shots, he later found out, through the bear's heart.

The grizzly did not appear to be fazed and commenced a charge downhill, directly at my dad. After more shots, the grizzly fell over, fifty feet from where Dad stood with his rifle.

The bear, which weighed a thousand pounds, was Dad's greatest hunt. And the

experience, he told me, brought the greatest
fear in his life.

I don't think I ever realized the power of
cancer. In my case it was so internal—the
grizzly inside. With every treatment, the bear
raised its head and charged, leaving behind a
weak and helpless person. Its raunchy breath
and gleaming eyes threatened life itself.

I usually came out of the linear accelerator
crying my eyes out. I'm not sure what it was
all about—the pain, fear, the uncertainty. The
exit dose of radiation was hot on my chest
like boiling water. My energy was left at zero.

My greatest hunt was at the Mayo Clinic.
I didn't have a custom left-hand bolt 300
Weatherby Magnum; nor was I the hunter.

I was the host, the hunting grounds
themselves. The weapon was the linear
accelerator.

On one day of treatment I decided that no
matter what the bear did, he could not reach
me, he could not tear at my heart. I would
not lose to the grizzly inside me.

*We have inner resources. We have never
called on many of them. Now is the time.
To be paralyzed by our disease is to forget
other powers that we have.*

Self talk is one of the best weapons we have in such situations. If we stop and think about it, we can recognize that we are constantly talking to ourselves, always carrying on conversations inside our heads. And when the great beast of our disease rises up and threatens our very life, that is the time for some serious self talk about defeating its charge, looking the beast in the eye and challenging it, using our fear to defeat its power. As men who have been raised in a society full of male competitiveness, now is the time to use that sense of competition to challenge the beast to the fight of a lifetime.

Maybe we can take the quiet words of Bob Dylan and use them for ourselves: "He who is not busy being born, is busy dying!"

Today is for living, for affirming our power to overcome, to win.

TEARS

It was November 12, the day after Veterans Day. I was back home after spending the holiday in Washington, D.C., but unaware of the events that were taking place there.

Because of the time change, I had difficulty sleeping. I got up at midnight and turned on the TV and found a recap of the Veterans Day events.

I was amazed at the pain that people were carrying. Men were in tears as they found the names of friends on the Vietnam Memorial. One nurse gave a particularly moving account of the last minutes she spent with a soldier in a Vietnam MASH unit. She said in her poem to the audience of veterans: "I was the last person he would feel, that he would know, both knowing that the inevitable would come soon."

Tears came to her eyes as they did to mine, which seemed to be the only appropriate response.

One of the stupid and cruel strictures that we grew up with in our culture is that "men don't cry." Misguided thinking about what it means to be a man lies behind this myth.

How many times as you watched a movie or a TV show have you wanted to shed a few tears, held them back, and then walked out of the theater or to the kitchen for a snack with a real pain in your chest from having stifled the tears? Why do we do this to ourselves?

There is an actual chemical reaction that occurs when we cry. Our bodies are getting rid of poisons. And when we cry tears of happiness, our tears cause reactions in our brains that release endorphins and help our whole system relax.

There is a message here that we shouldn't ignore.

Can we be strong and gentle at the same time? Of course we can. Can we be feeling men who can cry and hunt and fish and fix cars and play football? Yes. And can we cry when we are afraid and in pain and still be real men? Certainly.

I cried at the birth of my children, at the death of my brother in Vietnam, at seeing his name on the Wall, at my wife's death, at my remarriage ceremony.

Crying is a normal, natural function of being a human being. So let's turn the myth around: It takes a strong man to be able to cry.

Fish Story

Patrick had his head net on to protect against the bugs, a real lifesaver for a seven-year-old. As for myself, a little mosquito repellent, an old hat, and a focus on catching fish with Patrick was all I needed.

Patrick was a real trouper. He trailed about fifteen feet behind me all the time, taking four steps to my one, but on he went.

We waded our first set of rapids. He was unsure. He couldn't swim. I would have been unsure, too. So we held hands, walking up the stream together. The water was to my knees, past his thighs. He kept on going. He said, "Dad, this is fun." Music to my ears!

We approached my favorite trout run. I knew there was a nice brookie in there; he got off the last time. We crouched down, both of us sneaking up on the elusive trout.

I put his hand on my graphite rod and my hand on his. With a brief description of what we were going to do, I made my first false cast with him and then placed the fly where the fish was, all the while whispering to Patrick the play by play...he's got to be right there...and then—wham!—a nice fish. We set the hook. I fumbled around trying to strip line in while Patrick was reeling. At the same time I was reaching for the camera in my pocket.

When we finally landed the fish, I took it out of the net. We examined its color. Patrick touched its tail, and we let him go. My son put his hand in mine, and we walked to the next stretch.

Ah—the mystery, excitement and satisfaction of success. I was a lucky man. My body had held together long enough after my cancer to let my soul touch my son's. My fears had been put aside. I had succeeded in passing on a small part of me as I would like to be remembered.

He asked me why we had to leave the stream and go home. I explained that it was time to have lunch, talk about the day and start making up the story—all part of the process.

Most of us have wills with which we pass on to others the little pieces of our material life that are left after we die. That's fine and good.

Meanwhile, days go by and we miss passing on to others the pieces of the inside of us that will mean more to others than anything we might write in our wills.

There isn't a one of us who doesn't have some bit of living wisdom, some treasured part of ourselves, that we can share with someone else.

Sharing pieces of your soul, that which makes you uniquely you, is what is truly important.

We go around but once—and it's a short trip at that. How fine to let our soul touch another.

BROOKIES

A.J. McClane wrote a book titled *The Practical Fly Fisherman*. In the introduction, he tells a story of a man reminiscing about catching a trout as a young boy.

"In his youth the angler had looked upon the face of the river and it revealed nothing; it was a blanket of glare without depth or meaning. Boy-like, he probed the surface with inquisitive casts, hour after hour, sometimes in a gray mist when black twigs spilled droplets on the earth. Sometimes under the intense blue of a summer sky when bleached rocks lay bare, sometimes he probed when red-brown leaves spiraled down and floated in heavy mats on the water. The boy cast to the boulders and searched the rapids, and the maiden fish and the kelt passed him by. He followed the shore and watched the currents, as millions had before him; the length of the river was out of the compass of his time, but her depth was the soul of all men born to angling.

"And then one day he killed a trout, which he carefully washed clean and wrapped in ferns to bring to his father. The older man saw only a silent glassy-eyed creature, so the boy scrubbed it all the harder, running cold water over the skin while telling of the flaming gold and burnished silver—but his treasures never came back. His father, wise in the ways of a fly-fisher, knew that the color was simply a pigment, a trick played by the chromatophores, and that his son saw a fragment of time that belonged to him alone. Perhaps this was what the angler remembered as he lowered the net and shook his trout free."

Once, on a stream in northern Minnesota, I caught a nice brookie. It was about ten inches long. I hadn't caught that nice a fish for a long time. Usually I put the larger fish back, but I decided to keep it anyway.

I soon wished I hadn't, because as soon as I killed the fish the color went out of it.

When I was not able to walk well, I would find a stream that had a path. Even with a path, I would struggle along to somehow make it to a pool where I could cast and feel the healing power of the surroundings.

Cancer can do a lot of things to you, including taking your life. I felt that I had walked through the valley of death.

My cancer changed me.

After cancer, when I went to the river, rain falling from my hat, fly rod in hand, I realized I had the opportunity to absorb a little color, something I would spend the rest of my life trying to replenish.

Every one of us is going to die. Can't run from it. Can't escape the inevitable.

Thinking about dying is fine. But, as usual, we can overdo it when we are ill or in pain. We have to have perspective on this thing called death. We need to look it square in the face, see it for what it is, and keep on living.

Brook trout lose their color when they die. So do we. In the casket we are but a pale imitation of ourselves in real life.

I remember being at the funeral of a friend. Standing beside the casket, another friend looked at me and said, "He really looks dead." At that moment I felt like laughing and making some smart comment. The truth was, he really did look dead. So will you, and so will I. No color, pale, faded—just like the brookies.

But we ain't dead yet. And we have to grab hold of the everyday stuff that happens to us to keep us from just fading away into a pale imitation of our former selves. The trick is to put ourselves back into the water of life, to keep some color—at least on the inside.

FLIGHT 128

The flight started out like all others. I was in first class—a luxury earned through too many years of business travel—next to a man who had on cowboy boots and a leather jacket. He wore his long hair pulled back. As I got to know him, he told me that he owned a company that did chroming for a major motorcycle manufacturer.

As we taxied to the end of the runway, the usual niggling anxieties built up in my mind. Flying was tough. It took control out of my hands and put it into the hands of the flight crew.

Down the runway we went, and up, but only to about a thousand feet. I realized that we had no left engine and that the right one was going at a frantic pace. The flight attendant said we were going to make an emergency landing. All of the passengers got prepared with heads between legs. The attendant kept saying "prepare for impact," over and over.

I asked the stranger if he had ever looked at his boots so closely. He looked me in the eye and with total calm replied that he had been through a lot worse than this.

Moments later, after a relatively uneventful landing, we were on the ground and taxiing back to the terminal.

The man next to me had been a helicopter pilot in Vietnam. I had had cancer at the Mayo Clinic.

We both came back.

If there is one thing we hate as men, it is the feeling that we have no power or control over ourselves and others. We have grown up in a culture that has given us a misguided and untrue belief in our power.

When it comes right down to the nitty gritty, there is damned little that we can control. We certainly can't control illness or disease.

Sit back for a moment and reflect on how often you really ever had control. If you're like me, you'll begin to discover that power is really a myth.

And the other side of powerlessness? It is simply this: When we can accept how little control we really have, the power of our minds can help us stop worrying about what we can't control.

CHRONIC HUMOR

Humor was an important part of my early life. But there was nothing funny about my cancer.

I gave a speech once, outlining my journey, to cancer survivors in my community. I joked that I did not have chronic pain—or didn't admit it—but that my family thought I had a number of *other* chronic problems. The audience thought it was pretty funny.

But what was funny about tripping and falling, twisting my ribs, or having splitting headaches from back spasms, or having my feet feel like they were on fire even in winter weather? Nothing.

Was that life? Yes. Could that life be funny? Yes, somehow.

I think that many times I laughed as an option to crying. It was my choice to think of the possibilities of another day, maybe one with less of the bad.

I laughed because I had the end in mind, the finish. I had to believe that there would be a smile there. If not there—where?

Norman Cousins wrote a book a few years ago about how he laughed himself back into health using videotapes, books and movies. Maybe we all can't do that, but there is something incredibly healing about laughing.

In the middle of our pain or sickness or grief, to have a moment of genuine laughter is to escape if even for a few moments the steady hammering of what we are going through. That moment gets us out of the inside of ourselves, away from looking at our inner mirror of suffering.

Even to see the irony in our own illness or grief helps us to take a brief vacation from it and from ourselves.

So our prayer for today needs to be: "Higher Power, give me a chronic sense of humor." I would bet your Higher Power hasn't heard many prayers asking for that!

ME AND MY JOHN DEERE

Sports had been a big part of my life since childhood. Football, basketball, hockey—I liked the rugged ones. After my cancer, most of those went by the wayside.

With all those contact sports gone, what would replace the pads, the ball, the bat, the stick? Enter the John Deere tractor, a 1976 Deere with a single-stage blower and forty-two-inch deck.

It took the place of my snow shovel and helped me deal with a doctor-imposed twenty-five pound limit for lifting—definitely a problem in snow country.

The tractor also provided my entry into the John Deere community of men.

One day I stopped at the Deere dealer in Cannon Falls, Minnesota, on my way to my checkup in Rochester. They were super nice people and took the time to talk tractors. There were some old-timers there, and I felt like I was in good hands.

With my tractor, I could pull stumps, skid wood, and cruise my small property. That also gave me an excuse to put my leather gloves on. The leather smell stayed on my hands even after washing—perfect!

My wheel chains weighed 24.5 pounds; in fact, everything on the tractor weighed 24.5 pounds. (Groceries were still 25.5 pounds!) The smell of fuel and the hydraulic oil on my hands brought me back to a rugged feeling I had before my cancer.

My tractor became a lifesaver, an extension of me and my vision of myself. It was only a substitute for the action and tools of sports, but it worked.

As kids, most of us exercised an incredible amount of creativity in making toys, sleds, houses, guns, go-karts and the other accessories of boydom with whatever was at hand. We used our minds to create a world for ourselves. Along the way many of us lost that creative sense.

Now, in times when our activities are diminished, when our bodies don't let us do what we want them to do, it is time to reawaken the sense of play and put our creativity back to work for us.

One man I know escaped his disability by taking up whittling, something he hadn't done since he was a kid. His eagles, owls, bears, foxes and wolves became a way out of his feeling trapped, and yet he never left the wheelchair.

Another man I know created a set of handy tools for himself to help him get around the house. Another started writing stories for his children and was soon being asked for copies by boys and girls in the neighborhood.

How can I create new ways to fulfill my dreams? What can I do, what have I always wanted to do that will help me heal on the inside? Every one of us has the creativity to create new worlds for ourselves.

GRANDFATHER MOORE'S WOODSHED

No explanation of me would be complete without my grandfather. He was a great man. He was an old-time prospector, broad of shoulder. His word and handshake were as good as gold. He was trusted.

My grandfather had a soul. A soul that people could touch. I believe that his soul came from his surroundings, part of which was his woodshed. His woodshed was full of chain saws, double- and single-bit axes, and his favorite tools—the sledge hammer and steel wedge. He used to cut up fallen hundred-year-old white pine on his property and skid it to his woodshed with an old Willys Jeep.

I would watch him split the pine. A rich smell of pitch, leather, and steel would explode from each piece. He would burn pine cones and bark in an old potbellied stove to add to the flavor of his surroundings.

He passed away long ago, but every now and then I lay awake at night thinking of his soul, believing, because of our time shared together, that I share a part of him.

It was the woodshed that for me defined my grandfather. My woodshed could be my cancer, the thing that made me feel, that unlocked the inner me to be felt by others.

Often when we are vulnerable with illness or some other crisis, there comes a time when we as men turn inward and do some reflecting. These are the times when we touch the sacred in ourselves.

This has to do with our soul, with what we treasure about ourselves. And what we don't.

How do I treat myself? Am I driven by the values of success, full of little jealousies at someone else's accomplishments? Is competition so much a part of my life that even in the middle of my illness I find myself willing my body to heal itself faster or better than some other patient?

Or do I treasure the parts of myself that celebrate the victories of others, that support another who is in need? Do I have some serenity in my life? Do I have quiet times every day just for reflection?

Is there a higher power that I thank once in awhile? Do I have a quiet spiritual life that goes on underneath anything that is recognized as a public expression of religion?

Lots of questions. But as men, many of us have been so busy with the external part of ourselves that we have forgotten about that quiet core in each of us that nurtures the real us.

Being alone with our soul, reaching inside to learn about ourselves, is maybe the most important thing about our being human.

GRANDFATHER MIELKE'S GRIT

I got some of my grit from my grand-father. He could be a surly old man, not mean but a perfectionist—one hundred percent German.

As he got older, he became afraid of death. One of my last memories of him was of his last days of cutting wood. He had a small chain saw and a chair. He would cut a few pieces and then sit down and rest for a few minutes. He had a bad heart, but this technique worked.

I thought about the chair-and-rest system after my cancer and thought I would give it a try with raking. Raking requires some twisting and a lot of back. I couldn't twist, and my back was a mess. So I grabbed my chair and went out to the front lawn.

I'd rake for three minutes and sit for fifteen. While sitting, I could smell the leaves, feel the sun on my pale face and relax, knowing that doing anything is better than doing nothing.

It was perfect, though all I was doing was moving leaves from one area to another since there was no way I could bend down to pick them up.

My grandfather, I think, died in fear. I wanted to die in peace. The question was, where would that peace come from? My cancer gave me a clue, though I still couldn't claim to have the answer, other than to say it lay in living life the way I wanted to regardless of my situation.

My situation now included me, my rake and my chair—yup, buddies to the end.

A famous prayer is popular among people in all kinds of self-help groups. It goes like this:

God grant me the serenity to accept the things I cannot change, the courage to change the things I can, and the wisdom to know the difference.

I use this prayer a great deal in my daily life to help me protect my sanity from the craziness around me. When we are ill or in recovery there may well be a multitude of things we can't do anymore. One reaction is to get stuck in our anger or give up or get into a pity pit about how life has dealt us such a crummy hand.

Another possibility is to begin in small ways to grab hold of some things we once did, make our adjustments, and come to accept those things we cannot change.

Accepting our limitations, whether temporary or permanent, is not a task taken lightly given the way we as men talk ourselves into an angry lather about what we can't do anymore.

Learning to accept the things we cannot change means letting go of the past and having the wisdom to make choices for ourselves in the present.

COMMUTE

Before I returned to life on the North Shore, commuting in the big city was a twice-a-day experience for me. On one occasion, I was hustling along with the five o'clock rush hour on Friday as I left the metropolitan area of Minneapolis-St. Paul. Traffic was starting to move sixty to sixty-five miles per hour when up ahead I could see brake lights and cars swerving right and left. As I approached the area, I braked hard just as I noticed a dead grouse in the middle of the road.

Then my heart sank. In the middle with her were three chicks running in circles around her; two had already been hit. I swerved, but, looking in my rear view mirror at the hundreds of headlights coming behind me, I knew they would not survive.

That made me grateful for my inability to foretell the future. The sadness of life's normal events would keep me from fully experiencing life's mystery and the wonderment of my tomorrows.

Part of what it means to be human and a man is to experience sadness. Another part is to witness and accept mystery in our lives.

Sadness is not something we are comfortable with. But sadness is part and parcel of our lives. We need to learn to accept it, be with it, let it have its time inside us. And then we need to let it go.

But, and this is a big but, it is one thing to let ourselves experience sadness and another to totally lose ourselves in it. To get lost in our sadness is to lose perspective, to fail to see the little mysteries of every day that can also give us hope.

ON TOP

It had been four years since I had done
any real physical activity. Everything I did was
either too painful or required some motion
that was out of the question. I paid close
attention to what my doctors said. They
said I could walk, cross-country ski, or ride
a bike.

With little or no exercise, I was becoming
more frail as time went on. It got so bad that
I would wake up at night when I slept on my
side because I would get sore muscles from
sleeping in one position too long.

The Christmas of 1994 was different. I
decided to take that week off and go cross-
country skiing.

On my first day out, I walked into the
warming house along the trail and met an
older man named Charlie. He had a smile on
his face and told me that he had ten kilo-
meters in before nine a.m. Charlie was
seventy. I only felt like seventy.

At that moment I decided that Charlie
would be my inspiration. I wanted to find the
trail of Charlie and other men and get on
that trail and follow it to its end. So with
Charlie as my role model, off I went.

As a younger man I had been a good skier. After a hundred feet, I knew that had changed. Four years of dust, radiation, frustration, and fear came out of my lungs that first half kilometer. I was absolutely terrified of the hills. What if I fell? Well, I did fall. But every time I did I was able to get back up, shake the snow off, and move on. The trail that Charlie had skied was still ahead of me.

On the first day I hit the wall. It was a small hill. I tried and ended up on my knees, out of strength, out of heart, beat. It was just like being at home, just out of the hospital, when my only goal was to sit up in bed. The experience on the trail was no different in challenge. I just wanted to stay on my skis.

Two days and two failures later, I was still not on top, but getting close. I could feel Charlie's presence. He had gone before me, not with a tough-guy "I'm Number One" attitude, but as a man trying his hardest to make good with what he had.

Charlie told me that he was scared of some of the hills. He told me this with seventy years of life behind him.

His trail was easy to follow. I didn't know if I could make it to the top, but with

Charlie leading the way, trying the trip was all that counted.

Accepting limitations, but always stretching them a bit, takes guts.

Ride the stationary bike an extra half mile today. Take those crutches or that cane and go twenty steps farther today. Look around you and see other men who have had to do the same. They are all around us.

My dad can't climb mountains like he used to but he walks in the foothills of the Rocky Mountains every day. My friend Ed can't cut several cords of wood a day anymore, but he does a half cord. Jake is paralyzed from the waist down, but he is thinking of doing the wheelchair marathon.

We've got models all around us to give us courage to take the next step, to go through the next therapy, to learn to walk again.

We can call on that courage in all of us to get started and keep going.

MIKE

I did a lot of alpine skiing while I was in high school in Duluth. Since there was not much vertical drop in the area, we had to improvise for excitement. We built numerous jumps to do stunts we called Daffies, Backscratchers, Iron Crosses, and Space Walks. We did a lot of skiing under the lifts. The more trees the better, of course.

One of my favorite resorts was Lutsen, on the North Shore of Lake Superior. This area had many steep hills, and one in particular called KooKoo. That's where Mike came in. Mike always had some kind of cast on, but regardless of the plaster, he loved to bomb KooKoo. Yes, straight down, all tuck, no turns, no brake point. His attitude was point-them-down-the-hill.

He didn't always make it down without a crash, but that didn't deter him. He was apparently without fear.

What was it about Mike that allowed him to have no fear to the point where he said let's do it again—so determined to live that moment to the ultimate?

Right now—this day—is what I've got. Yesterday is gone forever, and tomorrow will bring its own experiences. But what am I doing with today?

What can I do to grab hold of some pieces of today and make something good out of them for myself?

I am reminded of a night several years ago when I was working with a group of unemployed men who were depressed, bored as hell, and feeling hopeless and helpless. They complained that there was nothing to do in our town that would get them out of themselves a little bit and that didn't cost money.

I finally got tired of their moaning and groaning and challenged us as a group to brainstorm as many things as we could that were free to do at all the seasons of the year. After two hours of amazing creativity, we had a list of over two hundred things to do!

Grab the moment.

BEEN THERE! DONE THAT!

As a young man, I spent a lot of time pushing myself, running my body through test after test to see what I could do. I spent many hours riding my bike at night down pitch- black roads, or skiing runs like Wildcat, Freefall, and Nasty Gash.

In the hospital, fighting cancer with surgery and radiation, I could move only my head. My healing led me to believe that those of us who had indulged in extremes in good health could come back during illness because of our full knowledge of the possibilities.

My cancer clawed me like the tiger, bit like the snake, subjected me to the cold of the arctic and the heat of the desert.

These thoughts came to me years later as I sat in my rocking chair, fire at my feet, coffee in hand. Fifteen below outside. Time to rest and maybe b.s. a bit.

Been there? Done that?

These phrases from today's young people usually come out in a kind of cynicism or world weariness. For us as men, they can mean something very different.

If you have been there and done that when it comes to surviving disease, illness, surgery, chemo, pain or loss, you have gained a settled feeling about having come through major crisis and learned from the process. "Been there" and "done that" can bring wisdom.

We don't often think of ourselves as wise men, but we are a resource for others if we wish to be. Wisdom-giving is a process of talking about "being there" and "having done that" and then reflecting on what we learned on that journey. Wisdom gets below the surface crap and gets at the guts of living.

I learned one thing after sixteen years of living with cancer with my wife. I learned some powerful things about myself. I learned about commitment, about hanging in, about not running when I wanted to. I learned about fear of abandonment, of loneliness. I learned a whole lot about my anger and how to deal with it. We all have our stories.

That is our wisdom.